Novels for Students, Volume 22

Project Editors: Sara Constantakis and Ira Mark Milne **Editorial**: Anne Marie Hacht

Rights Acquisition and Management: Sue Rudolph, Jessica Schultz, Timothy Sisler **Manufacturing**: Drew Kalasky

Imaging: Leitha Etheridge-Sims, Lezlie Light, Mike Logusz **Product Design**: Pamela A. E. Galbreath **Vendor Administration**: Civie Green

Product Manager: Meggin Condino

For more information, contact
Gale, an imprint of Cengage Learning
27500 Drake Rd.
Farmington Hills, MI 48331-3535
Or you can visit our Internet site at

editors or publisher. Errors brought to the attention of the publisher and verified to the satisfaction of the publisher will be corrected in future editions.

ISBN 0-7876-6945-8
ISSN 1094-3552

Printed in the United States of America
10 9 8 7 6 5 4 3 2 1

The Prime of Miss Jean Brodie

Muriel Spark 1961

Introduction

In her 1961 novel, *The Prime of Miss Jean Brodie*, Muriel Spark brings to life an eccentric, egocentric, and charming teacher in a private Edinburgh school during the 1930s. Miss Brodie's six students, known collectively as "the Brodie set," move through the grades. Miss Brodie sabotages school curriculum as she grandstands her own passions, both personal and academic. She colludes with her students regarding her status in the school and trouble she has with the headmistress. Miss Brodie is memorable for these students, recalled in their later lives, as repeated flash-forwards reveal.

Indeed, it is in putting this 1930s story in personal and historical perspective that some of its darker meaning emerges. In the pre–World War II days, autocratic, orderly, and foolish Miss Brodie is infatuated with Mussolini and Hitler. Inclined to think of herself as European, Miss Brodie praises fascism, her very taste for it a sign of her cultivation. Deluded by the appeal of absolute domination, with its apparent order and efficiency, Miss Brodie forgets that each person, however low and powerless, is a human being with rights. In her ridicule of Mary Macgregor, in her irresponsible direction to Joyce Emily Hammond to go off and fight for Franco, and in her attempt to sexually manipulate Rose Stanley, Miss Brodie sets morality aside and denies the humanity of her students. Mary's death in a fire in 1943 connects this denial to the greater obscenity occurring at the same time on the Continent in the death camps. In sum, readers are at first charmed and amused, and then jolted into pondering the serious, indeed dangerous, side of this nostalgic portrait of the 1930s and pubescent childhood.

Author Biography

Muriel Spark was born February 1, 1918, in Edinburgh, Scotland. She wrote poetry and worked at various editing jobs during the late 1930s and through the 1940s. In the mid-1950s, Spark became interested in Cardinal Newman's writings on Catholicism. With an English Presbyterian mother and a Jewish father, Spark felt somehow at a theological loss; Catholicism seemed to offer her a specific location or frame of reference, and she converted in 1954.

During the 1950s, Spark edited letters of the Brontës and co-edited letters of Mary Shelley and John Henry Newman. Her first novel, *The Comforters* appeared in 1957. Along with collections of short stories and poems, Spark published four more novels before she brought out her most famous novel, *The Prime of Miss Jean Brodie*, which first appeared in the *New Yorker*. This novel was published in England in 1961 and in the United States in 1962. Later, it was made into a play and then into a movie. Spark continued writing novels into the 1980s, often dealing with themes connected to religious conversion. Her 1981 novel, *Loitering with Intent*, deals with problems connected to autobiography and biography.

Muriel Spark lived in Central Africa during the years leading up to World War II. During that war, she resided in England and worked for the Foreign

Office. Ultimately she settled in Italy. She was married and divorced and had one child, a son.

Chapter 1

Boys on bikes talk to five sixteen-year-old, fourth-form school girls, who are distinguished from one another by the way they wear their panama hats. These girls, along with one other, form "the Brodie set," a select group formed six years before when they were Miss Brodie's elementary-level pupils.

In their conservative 1930s Edinburgh school, Miss Brodie is known for teaching unconventional subjects. Her students have heard of "Mussolini, the Italian Renaissance painters … and the word 'menarche.'" They count on their fingers, albeit quite accurately. Miss Brodie's set has by now adapted to the more orthodox curriculum of the upper grades, but they continue to be connected to each other through their friendship to their former teacher, whom the headmistress and others find highly suspicious. Miss Brodie boasts that she is "putting old heads on [their] young shoulders," and she affirms, "all [her] pupils are the crème de la crème."

Miss Brodie's set bears the imprint of their teacher and, like her, are famous, ostracized, and suspected of disloyalty. The set comprises Monica Douglas, a prefect and math expert; Rose Stanley, "famous for sex"; Eunice Gardiner, a "glamorous" swimmer and "spritely" gymnastics student; Sandy Stranger, "notorious for her small, almost nonexistent, eyes"; Sandy's best friend, Jenny Gray, known for her elocution and plans to become an actress; and finally, Mary Macgregor, the "silent lump, a nobody whom everybody could blame." The rich but delinquent Joyce Emily Hammond, a transfer student, tags along hoping in vain to become a member of the set.

Miss Brodie invites the set to dinner, revealing that there is "a new plot ... to force [her] to resign." These students are in her confidence, while other staff members are not. Some members of the faculty think Miss Brodie's style would fit a more progressive school, but Miss Brodie, who is in her "prime," is intent on remaining at Blaine, where she works as "a leaven in the lump." Like Julius Caesar, Spark writes, Miss Brodie can only be removed from her post by assassination.

Media Adaptations

- Adapted from the novel and based on a screenplay by Jay Presson, the film of *The Prime of Miss Jean Brodie*, starring Maggie Smith in the lead role, was released in 1968. In 1988, the novel was made available on audiocassette, and the film was reissued on VHS during the 1990s.

The chapter concludes with a history lesson that Miss Brodie gives this set six years earlier, when they are ten, she is forty, and the year is 1930. She tells them the story of her lover, Hugh, who was at that time twenty-two years of age (six years younger than Miss Brodie). Hugh was killed the week before Armistice in 1918. Hugh, a countryman, had proposed to Miss Brodie, anticipating that they would have a quiet life together. It is an autumn day when Miss Brodie tells the girls this story; sitting outside, the girls brush leaves from their hair. Hugh "fell like an autumn leaf," Miss Brodie says, making the girls cry. When the headmistress, Miss Mackay, approaches, the girls are silent. Later, Miss Brodie commends them for that, saying, "Speech is silver but silence is golden." The chapter ends with the poignant information that Mary Macgregor is to die at age twenty-three in a hotel fire.

Chapter 2

Mary Macgregor, right after the outbreak of

World War II, joins the Wrens. She continues to be clumsy and blamed. When she is deserted quickly by a new boyfriend, she looks back on her days in Miss Brodie's class as the only time when she was really happy. The poignant description of her death in a 1943 Cumberland hotel fire juxtaposes a moment in class when, as a ten-year-old, she is faulted for having spilled ink.

Sandy Stranger, on her tenth birthday, asks Jenny Gray to tea. Over pineapple and cream they discuss "the happiest days of [their] lives." Unlike Miss Brodie who has her prime, their parents got married and had sexual intercourse. The girls ponder the fact that the art teacher, Mr. Lloyd, "must have committed sex with his wife" because "he" has had a baby. Delighted to be left alone, the girls review their short story about Hugh Carruthers, Miss Brodie's fiancé, who was killed near the end of World War I. Sandy gets ink on her blouse and gets to go to the science room and have it removed by the beautiful Miss Lockhart.

Twenty-eight years later, in 1958, when Eunice is thirty-nine, she plans a return to Edinburgh and resolves to put flowers on Miss Brodie's grave. In conversation with her husband, Eunice reports that Miss Brodie was forced to retire, having been "betrayed by one of her own girls," and right after World War II she died. Eunice says Miss Brodie was "sane as anything" and "full of culture."

In 1931, Miss Brodie leads her eleven-year-old students on a long walk through the "reeking network of slums" called Old Town. Sandy has a fantasy about Alan Breck from *Kidnapped*. She realizes that the school group constitutes the body of which Miss Brodie is the head; like a divine injunction they stick together. If Sandy were nice to the always-criticized Mary, then Sandy would break apart this united group. It reminds her of Miss Brodie's admiration for Mussolini's troops. Lecturing about John Knox and Mary Queen of Scots, Miss Brodie seems oblivious to the signs of poverty in the street, to the street fight, and the obscene language directed toward the students. Sandy, who grows up to be the nun Sister Helena of the Transfiguration, always remembers the insight that "there were other people's Edinburgh quite different from hers."

Miss Brodie defines education: "*ex*, out, and *duco*, I lead… . To [her] education is a leading out of what is already there in the pupil's soul." She insists that she draws out what is in her students and does not put ideas in their heads. She has an appointment with the headmistress but is not worried. She affirms that her "methods cannot be condemned" because they are not "improper or subversive." After the walk, the girls are treated to tea at Miss Brodie's flat.

Chapter 3

The "most sexual year" for the Brodie set is 1931, their last year with Miss Brodie before moving into the senior level. During this year, Miss Brodie becomes the focus of the two male faculty members, Mr. Lloyd and Mr. Lowther. Monica Douglas catches Miss Brodie kissing the married art teacher, Mr. Lloyd, and Miss Brodie and Mr. Lowther are absent from school for two weeks during which time they become lovers. Jumping ahead to 1946, Miss Brodie tells Sandy over lunch about her attachment to these men.

In 1931, a man exposes himself to Jenny, who is later questioned by a female police officer. This woman, whom Sandy names Anne Grey, becomes the protagonist in one of Sandy's daydream fictions. Miss Brodie takes more interest in the music classes, and when she needs art books from Mr. Lloyd's room, she sends Rose for them. Sandy and Jenny notice that Rose is changed, that perhaps she has entered puberty. Later Miss Brodie speaks about her World War I lover, Hugh, who is now described as artistic. Jenny and Sandy amuse themselves by writing the correspondence between Mr. Lowther and Miss Brodie.

Chapter 4

The following school year (1932–1933) Miss Brodie's set advances to the senior level, all of them taking the classical curriculum except for Mary, who takes the modern. The girls perform Miss Lockhart's science experiments, and five of them study Greek while Mary studies German and Spanish. The headmistress divides the Brodie set and separately questions the girls, hoping to obtain incriminating information about Miss Brodie. One by one Miss Mackay's schemes fail. In the senior school, Sandy remarks that "There's not much time for sex research," and Jenny for one believes she is "past … her early sense of erotic wonder."

In late spring 1933, Mr. Lowther begins receiving the housekeeping services of the sewing teachers, Ellen and Alison Kerr; Miss Brodie takes a special interest in the job they do and intervenes in the kitchen. Miss Brodie attends church weekly, then goes to Mr. Lowther's house. The Brodie set visit her there, two at a time. During these visits, Miss Brodie questions the girls about Mr. Lloyd. She is glad to learn that Rose is sitting for Mr. Lloyd. In the summer, Ellen Kerr and Miss Gaunt inform the headmistress, Miss Mackay, about the nightdress under the pillow on Mr. Lowther's bed.

Miss Brodie vacations in Germany this year instead of Italy and returns to happily pronounce that Hitler is "a prophet-figure like Thomas Carlyle, and more reliable than Mussolini."

Chapter 5

Sandy examines Mr. Lloyd's paintings of Rose and thinks they all look like Miss Brodie. In one, Mr. Lloyd has overemphasized Rose's breast. Sandy sees paintings of Eunice and Monica, also. Paintings of Mr. Lloyd's wife and children do not look like Miss Brodie, but his paintings of the schoolgirls capture something of their teacher. Sandy insists with "near-blackmailing insolence" that Mr. Lloyd's paintings reveal his fixation on

Miss Brodie. Her attitude angers him, and he kisses Sandy intensely and then insults her.

As the girls become fourteen and fifteen, Miss Brodie confides in them about Mr. Lowther's devotion to her, along with his simultaneous consideration of one of the Kerr sisters as a possible mate. Miss Brodie wants to confide more completely in one of the girls, and she selects Sandy for her confidante. By the summer of 1935, Miss Brodie can remark that all of her ambitions are fixed on Sandy and on Rose, who continues to sit for Mr. Lloyd. Miss Brodie says Sandy has insight and Rose has instinct.

Sandy feels deprived of the religion of John Calvin, which shapes the worldviews of Miss Gaunt and the Kerr sisters, and she says Miss Brodie "had elected herself to grace … with … suicidal enchantment." She also concludes that Miss Brodie wants Rose to become Mr. Lloyd's lover and for Sandy "to act as informant on the affair." However, as it turns out, Rose only models for Mr. Lloyd, and Rose is the one who carries the information back when Sandy has sex with him. Miss Brodie focuses more on her aspirations for Rose and ignores Mr. Lowther. After several months, Mr. Lowther's engagement to Miss Lockwood is announced in the paper.

Chapter 6

At seventeen in 1937, the girls are still quizzed by the headmistress about Miss Brodie. They see

Miss Brodie as an "exciting woman." Though Mr. Lowther is happy with his wife, he continues to look at Miss Brodie with admiration. The new girl, Joyce Emily Hammond, also admires her. Taking Miss Brodie's political views to heart, Joyce Emily disappears from school, and six weeks later students learn that she has run away to Spain and died in a train accident.

In the final year, only four of the original six girls are still enrolled at Blaine School. Mary has left to study shorthand and Jenny has transferred to a drama school. The academic and professional futures of the four are described.

Speaking explicitly to Sandy, Miss Brodie predicts that "Rose and Teddy Lloyd will soon be lovers." Sandy, so full of fictions, realizes that this fantasy is not a game, not "unreal talk," but real manipulation. Sandy realizes Miss Brodie "was obsessed by the need for Rose to sleep with the man she herself was in love with." Sandy understands now that in truth Miss Brodie's dramatic posturing masks a real intention to play God in the lives of her students: "She thinks she is Providence ... she thinks she is the God of Calvin." Rose is not manipulated into becoming Mr. Lloyd's lover, however; she shakes "off Miss Brodie's influence as a dog shakes pond-water from its coat."

During the summer of 1938, Miss Brodie visits Austria and Germany and returns to announce the countries are "now magnificently organised." Sandy becomes Mr. Lloyd's lover, but from that relationship she values most his religion,

Catholicism; subsequently Sandy becomes a nun. In that senior year, when quizzed by Miss Mackay, Sandy directs the headmistress to shift from scrutinizing Miss Brodie's sex life to looking at her politics. Sandy says, "She's a born Fascist." Once revealed, this political position forces Miss Brodie to resign at the end of that school year. Ironically, as she wonders which of the students betrayed her, Miss Brodie tells Sandy that Sandy alone is "exempt from suspicion." To which Sandy replies: "If you did not betray us it is impossible that you could have been betrayed by us."

As a nun, Sandy publishes a book on psychology entitled *The Transfiguration of the Commonplace*. She is visited by people who admire the book and by other members of Miss Brodie's set. To a young man who visits, Sandy admits being influenced by her childhood teacher. Eunice lays flowers on Miss Brodie's grave. Monica asks Sandy about the betrayal, and Sandy asserts, "It's only possible to betray where loyalty is due."

Miss Jean Brodie

Miss Jean Brodie is an eccentric, egotistical, and idealistic lower-level teacher at the Marcia Blaine School for Girls in Edinburgh, Scotland. In the years leading up to World War II, Miss Brodie teaches in a theatrical manner and makes an impression on her prepubescent students, with whom she colludes in sabotaging the academic curriculum. Having lost her fiancé, Hugh Carruthers, in World War I, Miss Brodie becomes attached to the married art teacher, Mr. Lloyd, and because of his marital status, she diverts her sexual attention to the bachelor music teacher, Mr. Lowther. Miss Brodie loses her job at the school when one of her favorite group of students betrays her fascist political sentiments to the headmistress, Miss Mackay.

Hugh Carruthers

Hugh Carruthers, age twenty-two, is killed one week before Armistice in 1918. He was the fiancé of Miss Brodie. Sandy Stranger and Jenny Gray coauthor a romantic story about Hugh and Miss Brodie. After Miss Brodie develops attachments for the art teacher, Mr. Lloyd, and for the music teacher, Mr. Lowther, her stories about Hugh infuse his character with traits transparently borrowed from the other two men.

Monica Douglas

Good at math, likely to be angry, and with a red nose and fat legs, Monica Douglas is one of the Brodie set. Monica sees Miss Brodie kissing Mr. Lloyd in the art room and tells the other members of the set about it.

Eunice Gardiner

Small, neat Eunice Gardiner belongs to the Brodie set. She is well known for her skills in swimming and gymnastics. On a tiring day, Miss Brodie would ask Eunice to do a somersault in class to provide "comic relief." Later in life, in conversation with her husband, Eunice reports that Miss Brodie was "full of culture" and decides to locate the teacher's grave and lay flowers on it.

Miss Gaunt

Miss Gaunt, sister of a minister and not a fan of Miss Brodie, teaches the Brodie set while Miss Brodie is off, apparently ill for two weeks. Since Mr. Lowther is absent during the same period, Miss Gaunt theorizes that "Miss Brodie has the same complaint as Mr. Lowther."

Jenny Gray

Jenny Gray, one of the Brodie set, has

excellent elocution and plans to be an actress. While in the lower grades, Jenny is the best friend of Sandy Stranger. During the school year 1931–1932, Jenny is shocked when a man exposes himself to her. Later, she and Sandy Stranger make up stories about the female detective who comes to interview Jenny, and they amuse themselves by writing a correspondence between Miss Brodie and Mr. Lowther.

Joyce Emily Hammond

Joyce Emily Hammond is a rich outsider, a newcomer to the school. She hopes, perhaps by virtue of having two first names, to become a member of Miss Brodie's set. Later, Joyce Emily takes up Miss Brodie's suggestion to go to Spain to support Franco. Joyce Emily dies in a train wreck en route.

Alison Kerr

With her sister, Ellen, Allison Kerr teaches sewing at the Blaine School. The Kerr sisters volunteer to keep house for Mr. Lowther after school on weekdays and on Saturday mornings. The Kerrs are animated by their new role in serving Mr. Lowther, but Miss Brodie establishes her turf in his life by overseeing their cooking on Saturday morning and then spending the rest of the weekend with him, fattening him up.

Ellen Kerr

Miss Ellen Kerr is the older sister of Alison Kerr. When changing Mr. Lowther's bed linens, Ellen discovers a nightdress folded neatly under one of the pillows. She and Miss Gaunt take this information to the schoolmistress, Miss Mackay.

Mr. Theodore Lloyd

One-armed Teddy Lloyd is the senior girls' art teacher at the Blaine School. He and his wife have another child while Miss Brodie's set are ten years old. Thus, the girls know he "has committed sex." When the set are eleven, Monica Douglas claims she has seen Mr. Lloyd kissing Miss Brodie. Later, Mr. Lloyd paints several portraits of Rose Stanley, which Sandy Stranger says all look like Miss Brodie, and he has a sexual relationship with Sandy.

Miss Lockhart

Miss Lockhart is the Blaine School science teacher. She has short gray hair and a golfer's tan. She cleans ink out of the girls' blouses. When the ten-year-old girls get to visit the science room, they catch a glimpse of the chesty senior girls and the beautiful Miss Lockhart. After Miss Brodie loses interest in Mr. Lowther, he marries Miss Lockhart.

Mr. Gordon Lowther

Mr. Lowther is the music teacher for all grades

at the Blaine School. With Mr. Lloyd, Mr. Lowther is attracted sexually to Miss Brodie and is considered one of her allies. Mr. Lowther lives alone in his parents' home, receives housekeeping services from the Kerr sisters, and has a sexual relationship with Miss Brodie. When she loses interest in him, he marries Miss Lockhart.

Mary Macgregor

Mary Macgregor is "the last member of the [Brodie] set" for good reason. She is known as "a silent lump, a nobody whom everybody could blame." In the first chapter, a flash-forward informs readers that Mary dies in a hotel fire at the age of twenty-three. Later, when others know of her death, they look back on being cruel to Mary in school and wish they had been kinder.

Miss Mackay

Miss Mackay is headmistress of Marcia Blaine School for Girls. She "believes in the slogan 'Safety First,'" which is proven from Miss Brodie's point of view, by the picture of Stanley Baldwin, once prime minister, on Miss Mackay's office wall. A conservative educator, Miss Mackay suspects Miss Brodie's teaching methods divert from school policy and wishes Jean Brodie would resign.

Rose Stanley

Rose Stanley, one of the Brodie set, is "famous

for sex." She models for Mr. Lloyd, even in the nude. As Rose goes through puberty, her transformation makes a hit with schoolboys but she does not have the sexual relationship with Mr. Lloyd, the anticipation of which gives Miss Brodie vicarious pleasure.

Sandy Stranger

One of the Brodie set, Sandy Stranger is "notorious for her small, almost nonexistent, eyes" and "famous for her vowel sounds" which "in the Junior school, had enraptured Miss Brodie." Sandy would recite passages from Tennyson's "The Lady of Shalott," causing Miss Brodie to affirm: "Where there is no vision … the people perish." Sandy has the vision Miss Brodie lacks and, with her insight about Miss Brodie's effects on the girls, decides to stop Miss Brodie. Sandy reports to the headmistress that Miss Brodie is "a born Fascist." When she grows up, Sandy becomes a nun—Sister Helena of the Transfiguration—and publishes a well-received book on psychology.

Themes

Private School Education

The Prime of Miss Jean Brodie is set in a 1930s private school in Edinburgh. The interaction between the small staff, the personality of the headmistress, and the way teachers deal with students provide the framework for this novel's action. The kinds of social behavior and classroom decorum typical of this privileged class and setting are dramatized. While Miss Brodie insists on the girls walking with their heads up and keeping their sleeves neatly cuffed, she colludes with them to circumvent the curriculum and subvert the headmistress's authority. Pretending to teach the regular subjects of history and math, Miss Brodie instead elaborates on various unrelated topics, all of which are of great interest to her—her World War I fiancé, her vacations in Italy and Germany, her favorite Renaissance artists, along with information about cold cream treatment for skin and details about puberty. Her classroom is her stage, and Miss Brodie maintains that she is devoting her prime to her girls and that her girls are "the crème de la crème."

Topics for Further Study

- Research current law on the rights of students to disagree with their teacher or to protest school policy. Write an essay in which you evaluate those rights in light of the way your school handles dissent from students.

- Write a characterization of a teacher you had who left an impression on you. Specify what lessons you learned from this teacher and how your view and evaluation of the teacher has changed over the time since you were in the that class.

- Do some research about school clubs and the rules that determine membership. Write a paper in which you explore ways schools can be more democratic in their policies regarding groups.

- Write an essay on victimization, beginning with what it is and how it often occurs with prejudice and racism. Research people who fought against the Third Reich during World War II. You might investigate the Polish resistance movement in Warsaw, efforts by the Jews in the Warsaw ghetto to accumulate arms and fight back, and efforts at Auschwitz—for example, the successful detonation of one of the crematoria by camp prisoners.

Sexual Maturation

At ten and eleven, the prepubescent girls are curious and shy about sexual matters. They have a sketchy idea about sexual intercourse and make up scenarios about how it occurs. They conclude that since Mr. Lloyd's wife has had another baby, Mr. Lloyd "has committed sex" with her. Sandy Stranger sublimates her sexual interest into daydreams about fictional characters from *Kidnapped* and *Jane Eyre*. A man exposes himself to Jenny. Rose goes through puberty first and later becomes known among schoolboys for being sexy.

In the following couple of years, the girls begin to intuit Miss Brodie's sexual attachment for the art teacher, Mr. Lloyd, and her pursuit of the music teacher as a way of "working it off on Mr. Lowther."

Flash-forward passages describe the women these girls become. For example, Eunice speaks to her husband about her intention on their upcoming trip back to Edinburgh to locate and decorate Miss Brodie's grave, and in another instance Jenny, now married many years, suddenly feels erotic energy for a stranger in Italy.

Rose models nude for Mr. Lloyd and Sandy becomes his lover. In all, the novel economically maps out the movement through adolescence to sexual awareness and sexual roles.

Betrayal

Miss Brodie repeatedly affirms her commitment to her girls, the proof of which is that she is devoting the prime of her life to their education. She makes an impression on them, attaching them to her by taking them into her confidence. She attaches personally and inappropriately to a chosen group of six students, whom she treats to outings at the theater and invites to her home for tea. Yet, Miss Brodie is verbally abusive to Mary Macgregor; every time she berates Mary as a "stupid lump," Miss Brodie both betrays her responsibility as a teacher and denies Mary's humanity.

While espousing loyalty to her students, Miss Brodie habitually sabotages school policy and Miss

Mackay's authority. Miss Brodie is also quick to sense plots to get her to resign. Thus she "teaches" betrayal and distrust. When her chosen set of students are in their senior year, Miss Brodie is sufficiently obsessed with her frustrated attachment to Mr. Lloyd that she attempts to manipulate Rose into becoming his lover. That she is thus willing to treat a student like a surrogate object of vicarious sexual expression constitutes a serious breach of ethics. When Sandy "betrays" her teacher, she is only acting out what she has observed for years in Miss Brodie herself.

Victimization

Mary Macgregor is victimized at the Blaine School. She is ridiculed and scorned by Miss Brodie, and the other students follow suit, valuing their status with their teacher over being kind to Mary. Miss Brodie pushes innocent Mary out of art class, accusing her for instigating the misconduct begun by others. Miss Brodie and the students see Mary as a "stupid lump," a thing to be kicked around with impunity. Only knowledge of her untimely death at twenty-three causes her persecutors momentarily to regret the way they treated her. Mary Macgregor's victimization is a cue about the reality of fascist and Nazi racism and oppression. She dies in a fire in 1943, at the same time when millions of people are being reduced to ash in Nazi death camps. Thus, Mary's role and fate in the novel are poignant testimony to the effects of domination and subjugation. In another way, Joyce

Emily Hammond is also a victim. A rebel seeking a cause, Joyce Emily takes up Miss Brodie's irresponsible recommendation that she go off to Spain and fight for Franco. Joyce Emily dies in a train wreck en route.

Style

Repetition

Characterization of the Brodie set is achieved in part by repetition of the girls' famous traits. For example, Rose is "famous for sex," Sandy Stranger is "notorious for her small, almost nonexistent, eyes," and Mary Macgregor is famous for "being a silent lump, a nobody whom everybody could blame." When the character reappears in the text, the famous trait is repeated, like a tag or code for identification. This pattern has a humorous effect, but it also reduces the characters to two-dimensional figures like those in comic strips. As the story develops the traits become significant in other ways. Rose may be famous for sex, but she does not become sexually involved with Mr. Lloyd as Miss Brodie anticipates. Sandy may have nonexistent eyes, but she has insight enough to understand the dynamic at work between Miss Brodie and Mr. Lloyd and to see evidence of it in Mr. Lloyd's paintings. And Mary, though taken for a lump and victimized as a thing, is nonetheless a human being whose humanity is underscored by the description of her silent death. The image of her running back and forth in the hotel hallway, trapped in the fire and choked by smoke elicits compassion and undermines the comedy that works at her expense.

Treatment of Time

The story is told in chronological order covering the period from the fall of 1930 to the summer of 1939, yet at certain points the story suddenly leaps into the distant future, revealing important information that, in a more traditional story structure, would be withheld until it occurs in chronological order. In this way, the present of the novel is seen in contrast to the future, through the lens of retrospect it is reframed and can be reinterpreted. One example of how this technique works is in the several passages which show the students' later assessment of Miss Brodie: Mary Macgregor, at twenty-three and recently dropped by a boyfriend, looks back on her school years as her happiest time. Eunice tells her husband of twenty years that she intends on their return to Edinburgh to lay flowers on the grave of Miss Brodie because she was "full of culture." And Sandy, who betrays Miss Brodie and thus contributes to her being forced to resign, later admits that her career in psychology and success as an author results from the impression Miss Brodie made on her.

The Great Depression

The late 1920s and the decade of the 1930s witnessed a global economic depression. Prices inflated, currency lost its buying power, and millions of people lost their jobs. The New York Stock Market crash in late 1929 announced financial calamity to stockholders. Post–World War I Germany struggled to pay back its war debt from World War I, and unemployment in that country rose to almost 40 percent. The United Kingdom was less harshly hit by the depression. It witnessed unemployment increases during the 1920s but had in place government aid to address the problem. In *The Prime of Miss Jean Brodie*, Miss Brodie leads her students through the Old Town of Edinburgh where the streets are full of unemployed men, and where anger flares out at the sight of these privileged schoolgirls and their arrogant teacher.

Compare & Contrast

- **1930s–1940s:** By 1933, when Germany passes its own mandatory sterilization law for "defectives," the United States is the world leader in mandatory sterilization of institutionalized people. In the

United States some 30,000 are sterilized, all in institutions. In Germany during the 1930s, some 300,000 are sterilized in the attempt to ensure that traits like feeblemindedness (low IQ), pauperism (being poor), sexual promiscuity, and criminality are not passed on to the next generation.

Today: People with inherited diseases such as Huntington's disease and Alzheimer's disease may choose not to have children in order to avoid passing on this inheritable trait. However, in most cases, the state position is that this decision is a personal one.

- **1930s–1940s:** The science of eugenics in Europe and the United States theorizes that many ills besetting the human race can be eliminated. The trials at Nuremberg reveal the Nazi atrocities performed in the name of eugenics research and the manner in which sterilization evolved to euthanasia during Hitler's pursuit of the Final Solution.

Today: Genetically modified organisms (GMOs) and cloning offer benefits and dangers to food production in the United States and elsewhere in the world. Stem cell research is a contested issue and, as of 1999, the growing of human embryos for the purpose of using stem cells is illegal in the United States.

- **1930s–1940s:** In 1944, Raphael Lemkin publishes *Axis Rule in Occupied Europe*, which documents mass extermination and coins the word genocide. In one definition, genocide refers to the attempt to eradicate ethnic or cultural identity through mass murder. The Third Reich systematically murders at least 5.6 million European Jews, along with millions of other "undesirables" during World War II. **Today:** Human Rights Watch, Amnesty International, and Genocide Watch work to broaden the definition of genocide in order to include, for example, the mass murder of civilians by Stalin. These organizations also support an international tribunal where those accused of crimes against humanity can be brought to justice. In 1994, genocide occurs in Rwanda when extremist Hutus murder 500,000–1,000,000 people, mostly members of the Tutsi ethnic group.

The Rise of Fascism

Benito Mussolini (1883–1945) came to power in Italy in 1922 during a time of economic trouble and a pervasive sense that Italy had won World War I but had lost the peace. During the late 1920s, the fascist government intervened to save industries and increase employment. Gradually, Mussolini took more control of his government. At first he hesitated to support the election of Hitler in Germany, but by late 1936 cooperation was forming between Italy and Germany.

The Rise of National Socialism (Nazism)

Desperate for economic reprieve, humiliated by the outcome of World War I, and seeking easy answers, many Germans listened to the angry tirades of Adolf Hitler (1889–1945) who blamed the depression on the Jews and the Communists. Defying the Treaty of Versailles that prohibited Germany from building a military again, Hitler promised a stronger Germany through military power. The National Socialist Party, of which he was the head, was elected in the early 1930s. By 1933, Hitler was named chancellor, and soon afterward that he dissolved the government that elected him and became an absolute dictator. Nazism idealized the so-called Aryan race, while subjugating Jews and other unacceptable groups. Germany's grandeur was predicated on the extermination of European Jewry and the absolute domination of other European countries. With Mussolini's support, Hitler annexed Austria in 1938. World War II began when Germany invaded Poland in 1939; France and Great Britain then declared war on Germany.

Critical Overview

To say *The Prime of Miss Jean Brodie* was well received is an understatement. One of the finest works by the already well-established novelist Muriel Spark, this novel was heralded for its economic style, its charm and humor, and for its exploration of the dark side of idealism and commitment. Samuel Hynes, writing in *Commonweal*, stresses that the novel "is as good as anything Mrs. Spark has done… . It is intelligent, witty, and beautifully constructed." In describing the protagonist and her students, a reviewer for *Library Journal* remarks: "Miss Spark's account of the awakening and maturing of adolescent girls is realistic and at times amusing. Though the idol of their teens had feet of clay, she left an indelible mark on their lives." Finally, Granville Hicks, writing in *Saturday Review* affirms that Spark "proved herself to be highly talented and remarkably versatile." Compared to the likes of Evelyn Waugh and Iris Murdock, Spark is, according to Hicks, a writer who "goes her own way, and a fascinating way it is." The novel he concludes is "admirably written … extremely amusing, and deeply serious."

What Do I Read Next?

- In the novel *The Abbess of Crewe* (1974), Spark seems to parody the Watergate scandal, using an abbey instead of the White House and Abbess Alexander instead of former President Richard Nixon.

- In *The Girls of Slender Means* (1963), Spark writes about poor young women living in a boarding house during the summer of 1945 and their interaction with a cynical poet.

- In *Symposium* (1990), Spark tells the story of a dinner party. The butler gives the guest list to thieves who rob the guests' houses while they are away. During the dinner party, flashbacks reveal information regarding the guests' lives.

- Award-winning, twentieth-century playwright Lillian Hellman's longest-running play, *The Children's Hour* (1934), follows two women who run a private boarding school. When a delinquent pupil from an affluent, well-regarded family starts a rumor about the two headmistresses, tragedy ensues and the two women's lives are forever changed.

- In Rebecca Goldstein's *The Late-Summer Passion of a Woman of Mind* (1989), forty-six-year-old philosophy professor Eva Mueller is fixated on a twenty-year-old college student of hers. The relationship helps Eva confront her father's involvement with the Third Reich.

- Set in the Middle Ages, Sherryl Jordan's *The Raging Quiet* (1999) tells the story of Marnie, a woman who befriends the village outcast, Raven, a man people believe is insane but whom Marnie discovers is only deaf. Through a system of hand gestures, she is able to communicate with him. Then she is threatened with being ostracized, too. The novel explores the dangers in targeting people because they are different.

- In Theodore Weesner's *Novemberfest* (1994), a fifty-two-year-old professor of German at a New Hampshire college finds himself in a professional and personal crisis that causes him to relive a love relationship he had when he was stationed in Germany during the 1950s.

Sources

Hicks, Granville, "Treachery and the Teacher," in *Saturday Review*, January 20, 1962, p. 18.

Hynes, Samuel, Review of *The Prime of Miss Jean Brodie*, in *Commonweal*, February 23, 1962, p. 567.

Review of *The Prime of Miss Jean Brodie*, in *Library Journal*, January 1, 1962, p. 114.

Spark, Muriel, *The Prime of Miss Jean Brodie*, Harper-Collins, 1999.

Further Reading

Bottner, Barbara, *Let Me Tell You Everything*, Harper Collins, 1989.

> The main character in this story, Brogan, is a bright high school student, full of feminist ideas, when she develops a crush on her social studies teacher. The protagonist confronts the imminent divorce of her parents, and her trip through teenage angst is both humorous and thought-provoking.

Drabble, Margaret, *The Radiant Way*, Knopf, 1987.

> The ironic title of this novel comes from a children's primer that depicts life as peaceful and cooperative, which is not quite the experience of the novel's Cambridge University school chums from the 1950s who reconnect in London in the 1980s.

Newman, John Henry, *Apologia pro Vita Sua*, edited by Ian Ker, Penguin Books, 1994; new edition of work originally published by Longman, Green, Longman, Roberts, and Green, 1864.

> Newman accounts for his spiritual growth from youth through adulthood. A one-time Anglican, Newman converted to Catholicism in

1845, an event he discusses in this work.

Spark, Muriel, *Curriculum Vitae: An Autobiography*, Houghton Mifflin, 1993.

Spark credits the writings of Cardinal John Henry Newman with playing a significant role in her conversion to Catholicism, which plays an important role in her fiction.

Lightning Source UK Ltd.
Milton Keynes UK
UKHW02f1839080518
322302UK00009B/369/P